. Morgan, banker to a

D0947269

J. P. MORGAN
Banker to a Growing Nation

J. P. MORGAN
Banker to a Growing Nation

Jeremy Byman

MORGAN
REYNOLDS
Incorporated

620 South Elm Street, Suite 223
Greensboro, North Carolina 27406
http://www.morganreynolds.com

J. P. MORGAN: BANKER TO A GROWING NATION

Library of Congress Cataloging-in-Publication Data

Byman, Jeremy, 1944-
    J.P. Morgan, banker to a growing nation / Jeremy Byman.
        p. cm.
    Includes bibliographical references and index.
    ISBN 1-883846-60-9 (library binding)
        1. Morgan, J. Pierpont (John Pierpont), 1837-1913--Juvenile literature. 2.
Bankers--United States--Biography--Juvenile literature. 3. Capitalists and
financiers--United States--Biography--Juvenile literature. [1. Morgan, J. Pierpont (John
Pierpont), 1837-1913. 2. Bankers. 3. Capitalists and financiers. 4. United
States--Economic conditions--1865-1918.] I. Title.

HG2463.M6 B96 2001
332.1'092--dc21
[B]
2001016602

Printed in the United States of America
First Edition

Contents

John Pierpont Morgan, 1837-1913
(Courtesy of the Archives of The Pierpont Morgan Library, New York.
Reprinted with permission of Joanna T. Steichen.)

Chapter One

Banker's Son

To the American public of a century ago, the banker J. Pierpont Morgan was the most powerful businessman in the United States. He was the "Napoleon of finance." Because people around the world had entrusted their money to him to invest in America, his work in high finance—loaning the money to build American industry, organizing vast railroad and steel trusts, rescuing the U.S. from bankruptcy—was reported in newspapers everywhere, as were his friendships with kings and presidents. One observer said that when Morgan entered a room, "You felt something electric. He wasn't a terribly large man but he had a simply tremendous effect—he was the king."

Today, when the stock market goes into a tailspin, banks fail, or the economy slows down or heats up too fast, the Federal Reserve Board steps in and adjusts interest rates or provides a way for large banks and other private financial institutions to receive an infusion of cash. During Morgan's life there was no Federal Reserve Board; he was the "go to man" who stepped in to stop financial panics. By the end of his life, even Morgan's enemies agreed that he played a critical role in the nation's economic life. They decided to create the Federal Reserve System to institutionalize, under governmental power, the services that J.P. Morgan had performed during his career as the Baron of Wall Street.

John Pierpont Morgan was the descendant of two families that had arrived in America before the American Revolution. His mother's family, the Pierponts, had produced many famous clergymen, scholars, and politicians. One such politician was Aaron Burr, who served as Thomas Jefferson's vice president, shot Alexander Hamilton in a duel, and stood trial for treason. His maternal grandfather, John Pierpont, witnessed slavery firsthand as a tutor to the children of a wealthy South Carolina planter and later became a fiery abolitionist preacher. The Reverend Pierpont was contemptuous of businessmen, particularly those he referred to as "traders," and was not pleased when his daughter Juliet married Junius Spencer Morgan in 1836 and moved with him to Hartford, Connecticut.

The Morgans had prospered in business. Junius' father, Joseph, had started as an innkeeper but eventually became a "merchant banker," who raised money to loan to entrepreneurs to build steamships, some of the earliest railroads, bridges, and canals. He was a member of the Whig

Juliet Pierpont went against her parents' wishes when she married Junius Spencer Morgan. *(Courtesy of the Archives of The Pierpont Morgan Library, New York.)*

Party that warred against President Andrew Jackson during his two terms. Jackson, who feared what he viewed as a dangerous concentration of power in the hands of the wealthy few, shut down the national bank in 1831. Joseph favored the national bank because it could issue currency, lend money, help to sell government bonds, and generally stabilize the economy.

The need that was filled by the central bank did not vanish once the bank was gone. Ironically, by closing the bank Jackson gave even more economic power to investment bankers. Businessmen had to turn to private investment banks to receive financing, and the larger banks that could raise capital became even more powerful. But, unlike the national bank, these banks were privately owned and unregulated, which meant they had no one to answer to except shareholders and customers.

Junius Morgan started his career in a New York investment banking company before moving to Hartford, Connecticut, where he bought a partnership in Hartford's largest mercantile house. Howe, Mather & Co. financed the export of cotton on the clipper ships that sailed the Atlantic Ocean.

It was in Hartford, on April 17, 1837, that John Pierpont Morgan was born. Pierpont, as he was called, grew up a serious, temperamental, and sometimes high-spirited boy who suffered from all sorts of maladies—facial rashes called *acne rosacea*, headaches, and scarlet fever—which kept him out of school at times.

Pierpont followed his father, Junius Spencer Morgan, into a career as an investment banker. *(Courtesy of the Archives of The Pierpont Morgan Library, New York.)*

His father lectured him constantly on the necessity for hard work, caution, truthfulness, and prudence when dealing with money. One lesson he relentlessly drove into Pierpont's head was that nothing was more important to a businessman than his reputation.

Pierpont attended nine schools (mostly boarding schools), where he was notorious for his wild nature and indifference to his studies. He and his cousin spent most of their free time trying to get a look at the girls from neighboring schools. They eventually spoke to the girls when the chaperones were not around. Pierpont climbed trees to "converse with the fair damsels" in their rooms.

In the spring of 1850, Junius moved the family to Boston and started a new import business. Pierpont returned to one of his old schools, the Episcopal Academy, and finally began studying seriously. He played football and chess and studied Latin and Greek. Whenever he had a free afternoon he went fishing, riding or sailing, or watched ships in the harbor. He was developing other interests as well. In politics he favored his family's political party, the Whigs. He attended speeches by President Fillmore, the famous poet and essayist Oliver Wendell Holmes, and "temperance" (anti-alcohol) lecturers. He began following the debates at Episcopal conventions and collected autographs of famous clergymen and presidents. Eventually, he enrolled at a new high school, Boston English, which specialized in teaching math to young men preparing for business careers.

The Morgan children, 1847: Sarah Spencer, John Pierpont, Mary Lyman. *(Courtesy of the Archives of The Pierpont Morgan Library, New York.)*

Pierpont kept a detailed diary that listed his income and expenses, places he had lived, girls he liked, even the cost of postage on letters. He got a chance to put his interest in arithmetic and record keeping to better use when his father put the fourteen-year-old to work managing accounts, copying letters, converting currencies, and calculating interest rates and divisions of partnership profits.

Severe inflammatory rheumatism almost kept Pierpont from graduating with his Boston English class. During his sophomore year, he was sent abroad for several months to recover on the warm islands off the coast of Portugal called the Azores. Crossing the Atlantic, he kept detailed records of the barometric pressure, wind direction, distance traveled, and the ship's latitude and longitude. Once ashore, he improved rapidly, spending his days finding out everything he could about the ships in the harbor—who owned them, what they carried, how fast they traveled, how they were repaired. He wrote regularly to his family and was distressed to receive only a couple of letters in return. He also studied the poor people who lived on the island.

He recovered his health after four months and sailed to England to meet his parents. Junius was in London to meet with the American investment banker George Peabody. Peabody, who had moved to London decades earlier, specialized in locating worthwhile investment opportunities in America for British investors. He also helped the U.S.

government and several state governments sell their bonds on the British market. During his career in Britain, Peabody had become successful and influential. He arranged foreign financing for the first American railroads and other parts of the early stages of the industrial revolution. His role foreshadowed what Pierpont would do more expansively during the second half of the nineteenth century.

Peabody had no children and wanted to find a younger partner that he could pass the business onto someday. He heard about the talented Junius Morgan and asked him to come to London to talk over a possible partnership.

Junius took Pierpont on a tour of the city. London was the largest city in the world at that time and the center of international finance. Pierpont visited Buckingham Palace and Westminster Abbey, held five million dollars worth of gold bullion in his hands at the Bank of England, and attended services at Saint Paul's church. Junius and Peabody discussed becoming partners.

After returning to Boston, Pierpont was allowed to stay with his class even though he had missed an entire year's work. He had to work long hours to catch up in astronomy, theology, moral philosophy, and "Evidences of Christianity." He also managed to find time to attend lectures by many famous men of his day, including abolitionists Wendell Phillips and Henry Ward Beecher, Senator Edward Everett, and, once again, Oliver Wendell Holmes.

Chapter Two

Young Banker

In 1854, the same year that Pierpont graduated from Boston English, Junius joined Peabody's London firm. The new firm was known as Peabody, Morgan & Co.

It was a good time to be in investment banking. The British were growing dependent on American grain sales. The growth of the American grain business was made possible by the rapidly expanding rail network that had been developing since the 1830s. The railroads would need vast infusions of money to continue growing, and many wealthy British were eager to invest in the thriving U.S. economy.

Peabody, Morgan & Co. sold American railroad stocks and bonds to Europeans—taking a small percentage of the sale as their commission—and loaned money to American cotton exporters. Junius helped European investors determine the safest and most profitable investments. To encourage interest in America, Peabody had paid for the

American exhibit at the Crystal Palace Exhibition in London in 1851, so Europeans could see Cyrus McCormick's reaper and Samuel Colt's revolvers, among other items.

The Morgan family decided to move to London in the fall of the same year. Junius was grooming Pierpont to follow him into investment banking, where a family tie and a tradition of integrity were critical to getting securities accepted by strangers. According to the custom of the times, Pierpont's three sisters, Sarah, Mary, and Juliet, were not allowed to be in trade, and his younger brother, Junius, Jr., had died at age twelve. Pierpont was his father's only hope of keeping the family business alive.

Junius decided that Pierpont needed to become fluent in the foreign languages necessary for global business. He sent him to a boarding school on Lake Geneva, Switzerland, to study German. Pierpont stood out at his new school, in his polka-dot vests, bright cravats, and checkered pants. Letters from Junius constantly implored him to control his temper and be prepared to take on responsibility.

Pierpont hated the primitive dormitories at the boarding school and moved to a chalet, where his rooms became the headquarters for all the American students. He oversaw their recreation—playing cards and billiards, sleighing, hiking, and sailing. With their pooled allowances he bought them cigars, sausages, champagne, and American newspapers. Occasionally, they even studied. When Pierpont vacationed in Paris he bought nothing but the best—leather books, white kid gloves, a coat, a vest, pantaloons, collars, a beaver hat, and more cigars. He visited Versailles (the palace of French kings), Napoleon's tomb, and the Louvre museum. He was also forced to take a cure for an eruption of his *acne rosacea* at a hot springs, where sulfurous waters boiled out of the ground.

In spite of all these diversions, Pierpont proved to be a whiz at his studies. He learned how to translate three languages (French and German as well as English) and to calculate cube roots in his head. He advanced quickly through algebra and geometry to trigonometry and physics.

In 1856, at nineteen, he moved on to the University of Göttingen in Germany to brush up his German. He spent his free time at bowling alleys, billiard halls, garden concerts, beer fests, operas, fencing lessons, and dances. As always, he made sure to associate with the first families of the town and made friends in the student clubs.

Though he was enjoying himself at college in Europe, Pierpont closely followed events in America. Civil war between the North and the South became a real possibility. He and his father blamed the incumbent president, Franklin Pierce, for not keeping the pro-slavery forces in check and for failing to block the Kansas-Nebraska Act, which permitted the spread of slavery to the territories. The Whig Party had been torn apart on the slavery question. The Morgans now aligned themselves with the new Republican Party, which was formed to preserve the Union

George Peabody (pictured here) founded Peabody, Morgan & Co. with Junius Morgan.
(Courtesy of the Archives of The Pierpont Morgan Library, New York.)

and fight the expansion of slavery. The Republican Party was also committed to building railroads and other infrastructure that would help the nation's industries develop.

At the end of the school year, Pierpont moved back to London, helping out at the Peabody, Morgan & Co. offices. He watched as Peabody and Junius helped arrange the financing for the first transatlantic cable. The cable would take advantage of the newly invented telegraph and allow for quick transfer of messages across the Atlantic Ocean.

Those American markets—and the railroads that served them—were rapidly expanding. There were now twenty-two thousand miles of track between the Atlantic coast and the Great Lakes. Shipping freight from Chicago to New York, the most important port on the East Coast, took only three days, rather than the three weeks it had taken for wagons to make the trip. Trains could go across land, unlike steamboats and canal barges, and depart and arrive on a schedule.

The economic boom of the 1850s was also fueled by the influx of newly discovered California gold. Because money was backed by gold, this increase in the gold supply helped to pump more money into the economy. This increased liquidity made for easier credit, rising prices, and a rising stock market. High flying stock prices and higher interest paid on the railroads bonds made European investors even more eager to invest in U.S. railroads. Peabody, Morgan & Co. profited from the boom by serv-

J. Pierpont Morgan moved to London to help in his father's new business. *(Courtesy of the Archives of The Pierpont Morgan Library, New York.)*

ing as middlemen between Europeans and Americans. During this time of enthusiasm, though, Junius constantly emphasized how it was more important than ever that the investment house maintain its reputation for honesty and stability.

No economic expansion lasts forever, however. Pierpont had just moved to New York and started working on Wall Street as an unsalaried apprentice for Peabody, Morgan & Co. when the panic of 1857 brought the economic expansion to an end.

This was one of a series of panics that occurred in the nineteenth and early twentieth centuries. With each new panic it became clearer that the world's economies were becoming more interconnected. For instance, during the Crimean War, Russia faced a boycott by the allied powers of England, France, Austria, and Turkey. At the end of the war the boycott was lifted, and war-torn Russia desperately began to sell its grain cheaply to Europeans, undercutting American competitors. The slump in American grain sales slowed the traffic on U.S. railroads. As bond and stock prices dropped, the Europeans began to sell American holdings and direct their money back to London. This selling wave knocked down American stock prices even more, which in turn reduced the assets of banks that were holding stocks as collateral for loans. This forced banks to begin calling in loans in order to keep their loan-to-assets ratio within a safe boundary. These events represented a typical economic downturn.

To make matters worse, an accident at sea changed the downturn into a panic. In September 1857, a New York-bound ship, carrying $1.6 million in California gold, sank in a hurricane off Cape Hatteras, North Carolina. Because the nation was still on a gold standard, this caused a sharp contraction in the U.S. money supply. The already weakened economy convulsed. Stock prices collapsed, railroads went bankrupt, creditors demanded repayment of loans, overextended borrowers could not cover their debts, and banks and businesses failed. When the panic started to ripple across the Atlantic, the Bank of England took charge of the British crisis by lending money to reputable merchants and banks. This infusion of cash eased the restrictions. Peabody, Morgan & Co., with its huge exposure to American stocks and bonds, was hit particularly hard and had to be rescued by the Bank of England.

In the depression following the 1857 panic, hundreds of thousands of Americans lost their jobs. Newspapers and politicians looked for villains to blame and quickly found them on Wall Street. This scapegoating was easier than focusing on the inadequate banking system or foreign markets.

Undeterred by the economic slowdown, twenty-year-old Pierpont took a big chance with the company's money in 1859. While visiting New Orleans he learned of a boatload of Brazilian coffee that had arrived in port without a buyer. He bought the entire shipment and resold it at a quick profit. Although he made money, this was exactly the type of speculation that his father frowned upon. In retaliation, the firm refused to make him a partner. Junius agreed with the decision.

When he was not taking chances in the market, Pierpont was mingling with Manhattan's social elite. He was also spending a great deal of time with attractive Amelia "Memie" Sturges. When her father took her to Europe, Pierpont joined them. He began pressing her to marry him, but she held him off.

After returning to the United States in 1860, Pierpont went on a business tour of the South. He watched as cotton was loaded onto ships in Charleston harbor, where the badly divided Democratic Party split over the issue of slavery the same summer. The Republicans, at their convention in Chicago, nominated Abraham Lincoln.

Lincoln was elected president in November, and the Southern states started seceding one by one. Pierpont spent the spring and summer of 1861 handling cotton sales, railroad bonds, and Southern state bonds for Peabody, Morgan & Co. He also started sending news about government finances and the credit reliability of client companies to London, sometimes using the new transatlantic telegraph.

Late in the summer of 1861, twenty-four-year-old Pierpont, burly and handsome with a handlebar mustache, took part in a business deal that provoked years of controversy. He loaned money to men who were buying old government rifles, bringing them up to standard, and re-

Morgan married Amelia Sturges on October 7, 1861. *(Courtesy of the Archives of the Pierpont Morgan Library, New York.)*

selling them to the Union Army at a huge profit. He was accused of profiteering, as were many businessmen who sold goods to the Union Army during the war. Pierpont always claimed that he had merely made a loan available to a businessman and took a commission. Junius again thought Pierpont had shown bad judgment.

Pierpont gave little concern to the controversy. Memie had finally consented to marry him, but just as they began to make wedding plans, they learned that she had contracted tuberculosis, a disease that was incurable in 1861. Memie wanted to delay the wedding. Pierpont thought they should go ahead and get married and then honeymoon in a warm, restful climate.

They married on October 7, 1861. Memie was so weak that Pierpont had to carry his new bride downstairs and prop her up during the ceremony. Guests, afraid of catching the disease, watched the ceremony from a distance, through an open door. After the wedding, Pierpont carried his bride to a waiting carriage.

The newlyweds sailed for Europe, and Pierpont took loving care of Memie, carrying her in his arms around warm Mediterranean ports, hoping to restore her health. But Memie worsened. He hoped to the end that she would recover, but four months after their wedding, on February 17, 1862, Memie died in Nice, a city on the French Riviera. Pierpont was inconsolable.

Chapter Three

Family Business

In September 1862, still stunned by the loss of his wife and angry that his employers refused to make him a partner, Pierpont formed J. P. Morgan and Company. He traded government bonds and foreign exchange, financed commodity trades, and reported to London on American prices and politics. The war had suspended cotton exports and had also curtailed iron imports. Many foreign investors continued to dump American securities. In London, Peabody, Morgan & Co. was losing money. But after the Union victory at Antietam that September, European investors began returning to the American market.

Pierpont further angered the conservative Junius when he speculated in gold. Gold's value gyrated with each Union victory or defeat and critics charged that the traders took advantage of the Union's monetary troubles for private gain. Junius thought that Pierpont's gold speculations were evidence of "character flaws"—willful disobedience, recklessness, and greed. Junius decided that Pierpont needed firm paternal guidance and offered to make his son's new company his representative in America if Pierpont agreed to take on an older banker, who could keep an eye on him, as partner. Pierpont agreed, and soon Charles Dabney, a family friend and the member of a prestigious Philadelphia investment banking family, joined the firm, now called Dabney, Morgan & Co.

With the war raging, President Lincoln and the Republican Congress increased federal power through emergency laws. They gave public lands to railroad developers to hurry along the building of the transcontinental railroad, made federal lands available for homesteaders, imposed tariffs to protect industry from foreign competition, issued millions of dollars in paper currency, borrowed even more millions by selling government bonds, and created a national system of federally chartered banks that were answerable to the U.S. Treasury. These changes worked to the advantage of the investment bankers, who participated as middlemen in this new flurry of government-generated economic activity.

Pierpont chose to take advantage of a law that let him pay another man $300 to join the army in his place, but he would always be interested in the Civil War. He collected documents about the war, especially if they involved Lincoln—autographs, portraits, letters, legal papers, speech drafts, an 1863 message to Congress, plaster casts of Lincoln's hands, even the manuscript of a poem Lincoln had written in 1846. Despite his interest, he thought serving the fledging American business community was more important than serving in the army.

As the war was coming to an end in the spring of 1865, Pierpont was courting the tall and pretty Frances "Fanny" Louisa Tracy, the daughter of a successful lawyer. They married that summer and honeymooned in Europe.

The marriage was not a happy one. Fanny was a disappointment to Pierpont. While he liked the hustle and bustle of the city, she liked the quiet of the country. In 1866 their daughter Louisa was born, and a year later, their son John Pierpont, Junior, whom they called "Jack." There would be two more daughters, Anne and Juliet. In spite of the children, whom both parents loved, the marriage was not a success. Although the situation caused pain to both Pierpont and Fanny, divorce was socially unacceptable. They remained married for nearly fifty years, but managed to find ways to live separately during the majority of each one of those years.

At the war's end, Pierpont was busy fathering a family and trading in gold, cotton, iron rails, foreign exchange, government bonds, and commercial loans. Meanwhile, the nation's capital was being torn apart in the bitter struggle between the new president, Andrew Johnson, the conservative Democrat who had succeeded the assassinated Abraham Lincoln, and the radical Republicans who wanted the federal government to guarantee the vote and political equality of African Americans. The Republicans tried but failed to remove Johnson from office in December 1867. Pierpont went to Washington the same month as the impeachment vote was taken to plead for a return to the gold standard. The government had suspended the gold standard in order to print "greenbacks," or paper money, during the Civil War. The gold standard was a guarantee that paper money could always be traded for gold—a guarantee especially important to those who loaned money, because it meant that the loans would be repaid with money of constant value. Money backed by gold was not as likely to lose value because of inflation. This meant that a dollar loaned one year would be paid back by a dollar of the same value the next year. Farmers and other debtors liked greenbacks for exactly the opposite reason—they wanted money to inflate, or lose value, so they could pay off their debts with cheaper dollars.

This divide between supporters of the gold standard, or hard money, and those who supported soft money, or greenbacks, would be central to American politics for decades. The Republicans, who now represented the industrialists, pledged themselves in 1868 to the gold standard. They also agreed to impose high tariffs on imported goods as a way to protect American manufacturers from foreign competition. They nominated the former Union general-in-chief, Ulysses S. Grant, for president. The Democrats tried to attract the support of the small businessmen, farmers, and workers who had been left out of the Republican coalition. They also turned to the South

Morgan married Frances Louisa Tracy in 1865. The couple soon realized they had little in common. *(Courtesy of the Archives of The Pierpont Morgan Library, New York.)*

and promised to remove Federal troops from the region. When Grant won the presidential election in 1868, his treasury department tried to stabilize the nation's money markets and assumed some of the functions of a central bank. During all this controversy, Pierpont was not afraid to take time off from his duties if he thought his health required it. He took off the summer of 1868 and went to Europe by himself.

In 1869, Pierpont was off on another grand adventure, this time with his family. As soon as the transcontinental railroad was completed on May 10, 1869, Pierpont, Fanny, her sister, and his cousin rode west to experience first-hand the railroad that his company was helping to finance. They rode all the way across the country to Sacramento, California. When they met a group of Pawnee Indians, Fanny wrote in her diary that they were "just in from a fight with other Indians, riding the horses they had captured." She reported that they were "horrid looking wild creatures with no clothes to speak of—blankets & [knives] and spears . . . One came up and spoke to Pierpont, who, not understanding him, retired to the train immediately." The travelers stopped to see the Mormon leader Brigham Young in Utah, then returned to New York, having journeyed 6,000 miles.

The Pierponts were among the first people to experience the transformation that the railroads were bringing to the country. In the last decades of the nineteenth cen-

The Morgan children, from left to right: John Pierpont, Jr., Juliet, Louisa, and Anne.
(Courtesy of the Archives of The Pierpont Morgan Library, New York.)

tury, the largest rail network in the world would grow to over 70,000 miles of roads. During this same period, the West that had once seemed limitless would be settled. The labor force, fueled by immigration, would grow and huge domestic markets for agricultural and industrial products would be developed.

The millions of dollars needed to pay for all this construction and development was assembled by bankers like the Morgans and invested in machinery, factories, refineries, and mills. With no central bank to maintain U.S. credit abroad or to prevent panics and to stabilize the U.S. economy, the investment bankers had a quasi-official capacity. Companies, states, and nations had to borrow money from the bankers. For such large loans the banks would enter into "syndicates," in which many firms shared the profits and the risks.

To create this railroad network, land had to be bought, tracks laid, workers paid, and engines and cars bought long before the railroad could begin to make money. Pierpont and other investment bankers had to underwrite (guarantee) the investments.

But, as Pierpont quickly realized when he and Fanny returned from the West, some railroad promoters were promising investors too much, and others, like the notorious Jay Gould, were engaged in outright fraud. The fraud consisted of issuing phony stock, building shoddy tracks, bribing politicians, and stealing from company accounts. Another scheme was to begin building a parallel railroad

Railroad tycoon Jay Gould stifled competition by using fraudulent business practices.
(Courtesy of the Library of Congress.)

with the intention of extorting money from the existing road in exchange for a promise to stop construction. In the midst of this chicanery and confusion, it was usually the investment banker who had to move in and clean up the mess left behind.

Hoping to stop this ruthless competition which threatened the value of the railroads' stocks and bonds, Pierpont decided to try to minimize the cut-throat competition whenever he got a chance. He got his first opportunity to try to do so close to home, in the Hudson River Valley north of New York City.

In 1869, when he returned to New York from his transcontinental trip, Pierpont agreed to defend the railroad from a raid led by Jay Gould and another notorious Wall Street buccaneer named Jim Fisk. The Albany and Susquehanna was a small but important railroad because it connected to several other railroads and provided a critical link to the larger rail system for towns and farms in the Hudson River Valley.

Gould and Fisk began buying up stock in the road with the goal of securing a controlling interest. They were opposed by the president of the road, who retaliated by issuing thousands of new stock shares to investors who supported him. Morgan entered the battle by buying up the new shares and by hiring lawyers to help fight off the raiders. When Gould and Fisk claimed to own a controlling interest and brought in thugs to try to seize physical control of the road, station by station, Pierpont and his allies hired their own gang. The gangs fought a pitched battle with guns, knives, and sticks in a tunnel outside Albany.

Eventually, Pierpont won the battle over control of the Albany and Susquehanna. Then he persuaded the railroads to merge with another one, and Pierpont became an officer of the new company. This allowed him to have a say in how the line was run in the future.

The fight for control of the Albany and Susquehanna, when Pierpont was thirty-two, was the beginning of his long effort to guide the development of the rail network. His goal was to bring calmness and rationality to railroad building.

That same year Morgan began what would become nearly a half-century of involvement in the civic life of New York City when he joined Theodore Roosevelt, Senior, the father of the future president, to found the American Museum of Natural History. Two years later he became a patron of New York's new Metropolitan Museum of Art.

Pierpont was making $75,000 a year (today's equivalent is about $1,500,000). He and Fanny lived on Fortieth Street at Fifth Avenue in Manhattan, a fashionable address. He was already widely respected on Wall Street. One credit agency described him as being: "of excellent character, extra ability, shrewd, quick of perception, but oftentimes close and sometimes erratic in minor details which with his peculiar brusqueness of manner has made him and his house unpopular with many." Still, the House of Morgan had "rich and strong business friends and relations." It was also considered a conservative and safe institution.

When his senior partner, Charles Dabney, retired in 1871, Pierpont briefly considered retiring himself, citing the pressures of work. But Junius, who still exerted enormous influence in his life, arranged for Pierpont to go into business with Philadelphia financier Tony Drexel. He submitted to his father's wishes to form a new firm. But first he embarked on a fifteen-month European vacation. He traveled to Vienna and Rome before sailing up the Nile through Egypt for three weeks. During the rest of his working life he usually vacationed at least three months a year. He was able to complete a year's worth of work in nine months.

Chapter Four

Nation's Banker

By 1873, J. Pierpont Morgan had a national reputation. He was asked by the U.S. Treasury to create a syndicate of investors to help the federal government replace $300 million of high interest Civil War bonds with newly-issued bonds that paid out a lower interest rate.

Morgan got his first real test of his influence and savvy in September of that same year when he moved to stop a Wall Street panic caused by railroads defaulting on their debts. These liquidity problems had the potential to rapidly turn into panics and depressions because bank deposits were not insured. People and institutions that did business with the bank could lose all their money if a bank collapsed. So, at the first sign of trouble, frightened individuals and businesses began pulling their money out of banks. This was called a bank run, and it only aggravated a bad situation. What was needed at times like these were two things: cash and confidence.

The federal government was also hampered because it did not have the ability to intervene by increasing the money supply. Ever since the demise of the national bank, elected officials had few instruments available to deal with panics and other financial crises. The country's leaders had little choice but to turn to prominent and trusted bankers such as Morgan.

During the crisis, Pierpont became a kind of central bank. He arranged loans and imported money from England to ease the contraction. Eventually, his efforts were enough to end the panic. But he could do little to alleviate what was to become a six-year economic decline as demand for goods and services dried up and businesses responded by cutting wages and laying off employees. Railroad construction dropped precipitously as investment money disappeared. Ten thousand companies were wiped out in 1878 alone. Several banks and brokerages closed their doors.

During this period of the middle and late 1870s, Pierpont was careful about where he put his money. He knew better than anyone that a great deal of the "opportunities" to make investments were actually fraudulent schemes. Just as there was no central bank, there was little regulation of the stock market. The Securities and Exchange Commission, which today polices the financial markets, did not come into existence until the 1930s, following the Great Depression.

Morgan also differed from many of the other bankers and other wealthy men because he could be idealistic, as well as driven by profit, when he invested his money. In fact, he did not distinguish between the two. He was strong-willed, full of opinions, and self-confident, and he never hesitated to make quick decisions if they were necessary.

Like the London bankers he emulated, Morgan always wore the proper clothing—a bowler hat in winter, a panama hat in summer. At the office, sitting at his roll-top desk, he wore stiff-winged collars, ascots, and heavily starched shirts—trademarks of the serious banker. Only on sweltering days would he take off his coat.

During the workday he sat at a desk behind a glass partition in the big partners' room (there was a total of eighty employees), chewing on a cigar and growling out "yes" or "no" when someone asked him a question. He was brusque and impatient, and because he respected only those who worked hard and followed the rules, he had a low opinion of many outsiders. He disliked the press, rarely granted interviews, refused to be photographed, and warned employees not to talk to reporters. He immersed himself in every aspect of the bank, bragging that he could do a clerk's work without a moment's hesitation. Most importantly, he and his father had reputations as smart and honest bankers, and wealthy industrialists, such as Andrew Carnegie, the future steel billionaire, trusted him.

Morgan stayed away from the huge mansions of the newly rich that lined Fifth Avenue. He was concerned about associating with "gentlemen" rather than rich men. It was social class, not money, that counted. Well-educated, at ease with the wealthy and powerful, a member of the most prestigious clubs, he felt equally at home in Manhattan, Boston, Newport, London, Paris, Cairo, and Rome. But, unlike many of the sons of the wealthy, he was profession-ally driven. He worked hard. His life did not revolve around endless parties.

Pierpont belonged to nineteen private clubs, most of them restricted to Anglo-Saxon Christian men. He did not protest when wealthy Jews were "blackballed" from his clubs. Jews were also the one exception to his standard practice of bringing in partners and hiring employees based on their talent, energy, and competence rather than their social standing. He had been brought up with the casual anti-Semitism of the time, and it took him a long time to hire his first Jewish employee.

Unlike his own father, who had watched over every move he made, Pierpont tended to neglect his son. Jack was shy, delicate, and insecure, and never got the love he craved from Pierpont. After a Harvard education, he joined his father at the bank.

By age forty, Pierpont was a fierce-looking, heavy-set man with gray hair and a handlebar mustache. His huge nose was sometimes inflamed by the *acne rosacea* that had troubled him since childhood. The flaming red, pocked, and swollen nose made him insecure and contributed to his fiery stare. According to one story, the wife of one of Pierpont's business partners, trying hard not to mention his most prominent feature, got flustered as she served him tea and asked, "Mr. Morgan, do you take one lump or two in your nose?"

Pierpont accepted the common notion of the time that exercise was harmful, so he grew larger and larger. He even stopped lifting weights when a doctor told him never to exercise. He preferred cards at a club after work over tennis, where he sat puffing giant black cigars. He refrained from alcohol during the workday, but in the evening he had pre-dinner cocktails, wine with meals, and then a brandy or port afterward. Fanny hated the social whirl and stayed home, even when Pierpont traveled to Europe with their daughter Louisa.

Pierpont suffered his entire life from long, emotional depressions. He complained frequently that he wanted to retire from business. His marriage was unfulfilling, but his religion and social status did not permit divorce. Also, investors might be less willing to trust a banker who had divorced, and women who divorced were the object of scandal even if they were entirely innocent. So he maintained appearances and looked for female companionship outside of marriage. He sought out bright, self-possessed women who felt at home in the world and shared his social instincts and tastes. He also had other pursuits—travel, society, the Episcopal Church, history, and art.

Morgan contributed to hundreds of hospitals, museums, and other charities, and to the social welfare groups his minister, William Stephen Rainsford, recommended. Rainsford was committed to helping the poor immigrants who were flooding into the Lower East Side of Manhattan from all over the world. Pierpont gave over $1 million to erect a new building for the New York Lying-In Hospital, where nurses would provide poor pregnant women with food, milk, and prenatal care. He also made personal loans, usually without expectation of repayment.

Pierpont believed that ordinary people, the working class who were far beneath him socially, needed guidance from people like himself. He supported private organizations and revival meetings that tried to discourage immoral behavior.

The presidential election of 1876 was one of the closest in history. One of the issues in the election, again, was the monetary system. Should it be based exclusively on gold, or should silver be "monetized?" What should be the role of paper money? As always, Pierpont and his fellow bankers supported the "hard money" position of an exclusive gold standard. They said changing the standard would be a betrayal of European investors and others who expected to be paid back in hard money. The farmers and other debtors wanted "free coinage of silver" and cheap greenbacks.

The other hot issue was the role of railroads. Up to that point, all efforts by the railroads to form alliances to regulate prices and prevent competition had failed. Once an agreement to restrict trade was made, an individual railroad was tempted to increase its business by breaking the rules of the agreement.

Pierpont knew that the only way to control the regional

systems of railroads was to maintain actual ownership. This way, a single board of directors could maximize efficiency, minimize costs, coordinate information, and restrict competition. There were enormous financial benefits to the owners of trusts. Pierpont was determined to build a railroad trust.

There was strong opposition to trusts. No one wanted to pay monopoly prices, and farmers, workers, and small businessmen would be the ones most hurt when the rates to ship their goods were increased. Morgan had little fear, though, that government, either at the state or federal level, would stand in his way. It was an era when government intervention in business was politically unpopular. Even an 1877 Supreme Court decision that private enterprises operating in the public interest (such as railroads) could be subject to public regulation, did little to slow the organization of trusts.

The court decision certainly had little impact on a bloody strike that began later that year when the Baltimore & Ohio railroad cut wages. The strike begun by the B&O workers spread across the country as the workers demanded an eight-hour workday and the restoration of wages lost to pay cuts. Chicago and St. Louis were completely shut down by general strikes. Militiamen shot protesters gathered in the Pittsburgh rail yards and the crowd burned engines and cars in protest. After hundreds of deaths and injuries, President Hayes sent troops to put down the strike. The Great Strike ended in late July, but it left behind enormous anger—and revealed just how much the railroads were hated.

The next year, 1878, Congress required that some money be backed by silver. This move frightened the bankers, but the action expanded the money supply without producing social upheaval, such as had occurred during the Great Strike of 1877. This slight inflating of the currency eased the way for the return to the gold standard the next year.

Pierpont began to watch over the money supply. He would urge the U.S. Congress to increase or decrease the amount of currency in circulation depending on the situation as he determined it. Here again, a private banker was assuming the duties that would be formalized, under governmental control, when the Federal Reserve was created in 1913, the year of Pierpont's death.

In the 1880s, as the depression started by the 1873 panic ended, the financiers began to move their money out of government bonds and back into railroads. This mobilized vast sums. Much of the money was still coming from Europe, and Pierpont gave his European clients advice. His approval of an investment was critical to a railroad's success. He also exerted influence over the interlocking system of boards of directors and major stockholders of the railroads by bailing out bankrupt companies, firing and hiring managers, appointing new directors, fighting off hostile takeover attempts, and trying to damp down competition.

Pierpont finally reached the pinnacle of American finance in 1880 when he helped William Vanderbilt, heir to a vast fortune in New York Central Railroad stock, sell most of his holdings in order to avoid regulation by the New York state legislature. Pierpont managed to sell 250,000 shares without causing the stock price to fall—something that usually happens when a large block of shares comes onto the market. J.P. Morgan & Co.'s commission was $3 million. Pierpont also demanded a seat on the railroad's board of directors in order to represent his investors at the notoriously mismanaged railroad.

Pierpont escaped to Europe for six months during 1882. He also spent time in his beloved Egypt, visiting pyramids and temples and inspecting the mummy of Ramses the Great, the pharaoh from the Bible's book of Exodus. "I put my hand on Ramses' skull," he wrote to his wife. "His hair is still attached." Part of what drew him to Egypt was his fascination with sacred places and objects. The rituals and pageantry of contemporary Islam to remnants of early Christianity, Old Testament landscapes, and the ancient religious culture of the pharaohs fascinated him. One day his party, which included Junius, visited Jerusalem, and he saw the Church of the Holy Sepulcher, said to be built on the spot where Jesus' body was prepared for burial.

Back in New York, at his new home on Madison Avenue at 36th Street, Pierpont held court in his library that was so dark his servants called it the "black library." This mansion would become New York City's first electrically lighted private residence. Pierpont had helped finance Thomas

Edison's work on the electric light, and Edison returned the favor by wiring the Morgan home when he electrified downtown Manhattan in 1882. The offices were also wired and on September 4, 1882, Edison walked from his just-completed central power station to 23 Wall Street, which had been wired with 106 electric lamps. At precisely 3 p.m., Edison flipped a switch, and the Morgan bank became the first office in the world to be lighted electrically.

That same year, Pierpont bought an enormous steam-powered yacht, the *Corsair*, the largest, at 165 feet long, and most advanced in the country. He used it to escape from the strain of the office, his marriage, and his depression. When his family was staying at their country home on the Hudson, called Cragston, which he disliked, the yacht became his second home. He would dine on board and spend the night as it lay at anchor off Manhattan.

The boat was useful as a confidential meeting place to settle the endless rate wars, overbuilding, and labor disputes that plagued the railroad industry. A new problem developed along with the trusts. The new industrial giants, such as Andrew Carnegie in steel and John D. Rockefeller in oil, had forced the railroads to grant them highly favorable rates. This meant the small businessmen and farmers had to pay higher rates to make up the difference. The enraged farmers and businessmen began demanding that government regulate the railroads. Pierpont and his investors wanted to avoid government regulation.

In 1885 he brought the heads of the New York Central

Morgan joined the ranks of such great business leaders as the steel magnate, Andrew Carnegie. *(Courtesy of the Library of Congress.)*

and the Pennsylvania Railroad on board the yacht. The two roads had been locked in a rate war. While the *Corsair* sailed up and down the Hudson, he sat under the rear awning, flanked by the railroad chiefs, smoking his huge black cigars. He stressed the displeasure of European investors with American railroads, but mostly sat by and let the railway men debate among themselves, occasionally suggesting ideas. He did make the point, repeatedly, that if they could not govern themselves then the U.S. government would. He kept them until evening, when they finally agreed to buy out each other's adjacent lines and to cease their destructive competition. The agreement became known in the newspapers as the Great Railroad Treaty of 1885, or the Corsair Compact. The newspapers lionized Pierpont. Even his father had nothing but praise for his forty-eight-year-old son's achievement.

But the Corsair Compact was only the beginning. Other railroads continued the brutal fights during the 1880s. Then, in 1887 Congress passed the Interstate Commerce Act, which formed the Interstate Commerce Commission (ICC). This was the first federal regulatory commission. It formally forbade railroads to discriminate among shippers, required them to publish schedules of fares, outlawed preferential rebates, prohibited price-fixing, and determined "just and reasonable" rates. Supporters of the act included the small shippers and the railroads themselves, who hoped it would provide stability. Junius opposed the new law, and Pierpont did not like it but, always practical, resolved to work with it. The ICC lacked any real power, however, and Congress was not inclined to give it more, so the rebates continued.

In December 1888, as newspaper reporters waited outside, Pierpont arranged a meeting of western railroad presidents and bankers at his home. In the "black library," Pierpont told them that they could "no longer take the law into their own hands." He told the railroad heads that if they avoided rate-cutting, secret deals, and cut-throat competition, the bankers would agree to not finance the construction of competing railways. The presidents agreed on a sixty-day truce. The next month, Pierpont oversaw another agreement in his library to regulate the entire rail system by setting rates, arbitrating disputes, and fining offenders. The idea was to create a cartel that would not anger the Interstate Commerce Commission.

But eventually the agreements failed, and the rate wars came back, especially in the West. Pierpont decided to try one last time. In December 1890, he proposed to establish a group to set uniform rates. He bragged to a reporter, "Think of it—all the competing traffic of the roads west of Chicago and St. Louis placed in the control of about thirty men!" It made perfect sense to him that the roads should be controlled by businessmen such as himself. The newspapers were not so kind. One headline blared, "Railroad Kings Form a Gigantic Trust." As it turned out, it was a waste of time. Even this plan failed, as members of the trust cheated and newcomers cut rates and won new business. There simply were not enough passengers and freight shipments for the debt-ridden railroads.

Chapter Five

Dodging a Panic

Junius Morgan died in 1890 of injuries sustained in a carriage accident. He was seventy-seven. Pierpont mourned his father for months and paid tribute with elaborate memorials, including several buildings he funded that were named for his father at the Harvard Medical School.

Pierpont inherited $15 million, doubling his personal fortune overnight. One of the first things he did was to give a naval architect a free hand to design the largest private pleasure vessel afloat—the luxurious, 241-foot *Corsair II.* The only requirement was that it be able to turn about in the Hudson River near Cragston.

That same year, three years after Congress began trying to regulate the railroads with the Interstate Commerce Act, it passed the Sherman Antitrust Act. The intent of the bill was to control huge trusts, such as Standard Oil, that had developed over the past two decades. Its supporters hoped that the new law, which prohibited "restraints of trade," would prevent the trusts from driving competitors out of business, destroying locally-owned businesses, extracting rebates, and bribing politicians.

The Sherman Act's opponents, among them Pierpont, argued that the U.S. was no longer a nation of farmers and small producers. America had been drastically reshaped by developments in transportation (the railroads), communications (the telephone), and industrial productivity. It was now a country of mass production and distribution, which efficiently delivered vast amounts of goods at declining costs. Private enterprise was responsible for all this, they said, and regulation would merely sap the energy from industrial development.

The Sherman Antitrust Act did little to stop the trusts—at first. It was difficult to determine exactly what the law required. Which trade restraints were illegal: price fixing, mergers, or cartels? When did an agreement actually restrain trade? What was an illegal monopoly act? What was a specific, legal definition of a trust? None of these questions were answered in the law. It was left up to the Supreme Court to interpret the Sherman Act. In the early decades the conservative Supreme Court interpreted the law narrowly and confusingly. It outlawed cartels, for example, but permitted the buying up of companies. An unintended consequence of the Act was that the high court used it to outlaw organized labor as a cartel. Strikes were interpreted as restraints of trade.

The election of November 1892 returned Grover Cleveland to the presidency after four years out of office. Though Morgan was a Republican and Cleveland a Democrat, Pierpont supported Cleveland because the new president was for "sound money," that is, the gold standard, which meant that the government could pay out gold for paper money. The Republican Congress favored "free coinage" of silver.

Cleveland had just taken office when a new stock market panic in May 1893 touched off one of the worst depressions in U.S. history. A financial panic started a run on the banks and over 600 failed. Thousands of factories, mills, and railroads went bankrupt, tens of thousands of people lost jobs, and the already declining price of farm crops fell faster.

Hoping to deal with the crisis, Congress actually made the situation worse. Over the objections of Congressman William Jennings Bryan and others, Congress voted to "demonetize" silver—that is, they removed it as backing for money. The goal was to stop the hoarding of gold, which resulted from fear that silver money would soon be worthless. But the change came too late and the drain of gold from the treasury continued. As a result of hoarding and the newly restricted money supply caused by the demonetization of silver, cash grew so scarce that brokers traded it on Wall Street at curbside.

As railroads failed, Pierpont assumed control over many of them because they had been used as "collateral," or backing, for loans. He began reorganizing them into

This political sketch satirizes the titans of nineteenth-century business that legislation such as the Sherman Antitrust Act was designed to control. Banker J. P. Morgan, with his characteristic top hat, is on the left. Oil baron John D. Rockefeller is in the middle, and to the right is industrialist Andrew Mellon. *(Courtesy of the Library of Congress.)*

regional consolidations— "Morganizing" them, as it was called. He took over the Erie, the Chesapeake and Ohio, the Philadelphia and Reading, the Santa Fe, the Northern Pacific, the Great Northern, the New York, the Lehigh Valley, the Jersey Central, and the Southern Railway. When he was finished, the newly reorganized railroads were far more efficient and profitable. By 1900, the nation's many railroads were consolidated into six large systems.

In 1895, during the long depression that followed the 1893 panic, Pierpont engineered his most dazzling feat yet: He saved the gold standard and briefly controlled the flow of gold into and out of the United States.

Congress's demonetizing of silver had not stopped the gold drain. Investors traded in their dollars for bullion and shipped it to Europe. European bankers feared that Bryan and his populist forces would bring silver money, or greenbacks, back into circulation. This would undermine the gold standard. At the same time, the railroads did not lower shipping prices. The farmers faced ruin, caught between the falling prices they received for their goods and the high shipping costs they had to pay to get their goods to market. Because he was the financier of the railroads, J.P. Morgan was soon the symbol of the heartless money man and agent of foreign gold who was determined to suck the life blood out of the small farmer or businessman. Pierpont thought that protecting his clients' investments was the best thing he could do to protect the future prosperity of everyone. If the investors took huge

William Jenning Bryan's "Cross of Gold" speech argued against the gold standard, which he believed hurt the poor and working classes. *(Courtesy of the Library of Congress.)*

losses in the United States, especially if those losses were the result of governmental changes, it could be years, even decades, before they were again willing to invest in the United States.

The immediate problem was a fear that the U.S. Government might not be able to redeem the paper money for gold because there was not enough in storage. When Cleveland could not persuade Congress to sell bonds for gold in order to increase the gold supply, Pierpont proposed at a White House meeting that his bank create a syndicate to sell European and American gold to the government in return for bonds. Using an emergency law passed during the Civil War, he would be given permission to buy gold for the government. He promised that once it was purchased he would make sure that it did not flow out of the country. Again, he was volunteering to do the government's work.

Although the bonds were risky, they sold out quickly, due in large measure on Pierpont's word. This not only stopped the run on gold, it allowed the Treasury to replace the gold that had been drawn out at the beginning of the panic.

The Populists and many newspapers were aghast at what they saw as capitulation to "Jewish bankers and British gold." Bryan vehemently denounced the bond-for-gold deal in Congress. They ignored the fact that Morgan's plan had ended a financial panic.

Cleveland's participation in Morgan's effort to end the

gold crisis angered many in his own party. At the 1896 Democratic Convention, the Democrats rejected Cleveland and nominated William Jennings Bryan of Nebraska to run for president. Accepting the nomination, Bryan, who was also the nominee of the new Populist Party, gave his famous "Cross of Gold" speech: "You shall not press down upon the brow of labor this crown of thorns, you shall not crucify mankind upon a cross of gold." He also attacked Morgan and the other bankers.

In the 1896 election, Republican William McKinley, a former congressman and governor of Ohio, defeated Bryan by receiving fifty-two percent of the votes, with the help of many Northern and Eastern Democrats who deserted their party and joined the Republicans. During the campaign, Pierpont had lobbied for a gold standard plank in the Republican party platform. He entertained Mark Hanna, Ohio banker and chairman of the Republican National committee, aboard the *Corsair II.* The new president supported the gold standard and four years later signed a law re-establishing it.

Chapter Six

Art Collector

As Pierpont entered his sixties, he spent less time at the bank, often sending in instructions by telegram. He devoted more time to what was becoming his first love—art collecting. At first, he concentrated on books and manuscripts and letters of British royalty, storing them in his Madison Avenue basement. Soon they were heaped on chairs and stacked in corners. He could not keep track of them. Other works gathered dust in the vaults of the office at 23 Wall Street and in a warehouse.

He intended to leave his collections for the "instruction and pleasure" of the American people and asked in his will that they be made "permanently available" to the public. He built a library that looked like a marble Italian Renaissance palace for the manuscripts and rare books and moved his collection into it in 1906.

By the time his library was completed he had enlarged his scope beyond manuscripts to become one of the world's premier art collectors. He sometimes bought entire collections. He made most of his purchases from impoverished European aristocrats who were selling family heirlooms that included the great works of previous centuries.

Morgan commissioned experts to find him the best works of art and literature that were available for purchase. Among his treasures were Napoleon's watch, Leonardo da Vinci's notebooks, Catherine the Great's snuff box, jewelry of the Medici family from Renaissance Florence, Shakespearean first folios, a five page letter of George Washington's, and Roman coins showing the heads of all twelve Caesars but one. He developed a diverse collection—Egyptian, Greek, and Latin papyrus rolls, medieval vellum codes, the first volumes printed with the invention of movable type by Johann Gutenberg, etchings by Rembrandt, Dürer prints, the original manuscript of Dickens' *A Christmas Carol*, portrait miniatures, vases, enamels, reliquary caskets, letters signed by famous people, royal marriage contracts, Old Master paintings and drawings, sculpture, tapestries, furniture, bronzes, jewelry, watches, coins, armor, seventeenth-century German metal work, gold carvings, rare books, Babylonian cylinder seals, Assyrian reliefs, Roman frescoes, jewel-encrusted books, gilded altarpieces, illuminated manuscripts, gold and silver cups, porcelains, and ivory.

When he bought the portrait miniatures, Pierpont was realizing a long term dream. Fascinated since childhood with European history and royalty, Pierpont now owned objects once handled by Queen Elizabeth I, King Henry VIII, Napoleon, Lord Nelson, and ladies of the French court.

He knew that to create a big collection he had to buy art in huge batches and then add to them as good pieces became available. Throughout Europe, Morgan's arrival brought art dealers, booksellers, and antiquarians flocking to see him. He was proud of his holdings and commissioned art historians to assemble illustrated catalogues. He subsidized their printing and distribution to the royal households of Europe and to libraries around the country.

Pierpont typically bought art on credit. His purchases consumed so much money that his partners complained that vast sums were being "lost" which could have been invested in the bank. Usually paying the asking price, he never bargained for things he wanted. His acquisitions helped drive the art market to new heights.

Buying more works of art and literature than he could properly house, Pierpont began to donate them to museums. He gave the just-completed New York Public Library a collection of manuscripts, letters, and books that included correspondence by Noah Webster, Horace Greeley, and presidents Andrew Jackson and James Monroe. He gave two thousand Chinese porcelains and a huge collection of medieval battle armor to the Metropolitan Museum of Art. Later, as president of the Museum, he oversaw the creation of new departments, hired experts to curate them, funded archaeological excavations, and donated sums large enough to attract other contributions.

In addition to collecting art, Morgan also helped to fund public buildings, such as Madison Square Garden. *(Courtesy of the Archives of The Pierpont Morgan Library, New York.)*

Pierpont pursued other interests as well. He bought a cottage in Newport, Rhode Island, an apartment on Jekyll Island off the Georgia coast, and a wooded camp in the Adirondack Mountains of upstate New York. While in the mountains he kept an engine waiting at the nearby train station twenty-four hours a day, steamed up and ready to go, in case he had to leave on a moment's notice for New York. When Pierpont threw parties at the mountain camp, he would bring up a private railroad car full of friends and a baggage car loaded with racks of vintage champagne.

As commodore of the New York Yacht Club, he financed "Morgan" cup races and helped pay for the *Columbia*, which defended the America's Cup in October 1899. The event was one of the first "covered" by Guglielmo Marconi, the inventor of the "wireless telegraph," or radio.

In 1898, over his heated protests, the Navy had conscripted *Corsair II* for use in the Spanish-American War. He had opposed the war because of fears it would damage international trade. The Navy paid Pierpont $225,000 for the ship and transformed it into the gunboat *Gloucester*. It saw action in the Battle of Santiago and was damaged by a Spanish shell. Pierpont kept a piece of the ship's splintered mast as a memento. He had a new *Corsair III* built, a faithful, but larger, reproduction of *Corsair II*. Three hundred feet long and requiring a crew of seventy, the new yacht could cross the Atlantic. He usually sent it and the crew ahead while he sailed to Europe on White Star liners.

Upon arrival in Europe, he could take friends cruising in the Mediterranean or along the Italian coast, or join Europe's crowned heads for sailing races. At the end of these trips, *Corsair III* preceded him home, then steamed out to pick him up in New York Harbor.

Chapter Seven

U.S. Steel

On December 12, 1900, Pierpont attended a dinner given to honor Charles Schwab, the president of Andrew Carnegie's steel company. In his speech, Schwab talked eloquently of how profitable a giant steel trust would be. He argued that only a trust could distribute both raw and manufactured steel products in a way that matched supply and demand efficiently.

Earlier, Morgan had helped some investors organize the Federated Steel Company, which presented the first real challenge to the dominance of Carnegie Steel. Carnegie had not ignored the challenge and was busy building a new factory that threatened to undersell Federated Steel. The steel business faced the prospect of the same intense competitive war that had been so destructive to the railroads.

Pierpont correctly determined that Schwab's speech was intended as an offer to Morgan and his investors to find a way to merge their companies into a steel trust.

Pierpont called for a meeting of Schwab and the Federated Steel investors to be held at his home. There he worked out a proposal in an all-night session in the "black library" to develop U.S. Steel, a new company that would control more than half the world's steel business.

Andrew Carnegie had to be brought into the arrangement. Carnegie, a Scottish immigrant who had risen from poverty to be one of the world's wealthiest men, was now in his sixties and had mentioned retiring. He wanted to begin finding ways to give his money away. When Schwab, at Morgan's request, approached Carnegie about selling his interest in Carnegie Steel in order to form the trust, the tough Scot asked for $480 million for his company. When Schwab delivered a slip of paper with the price and the demand that it be paid in bonds, not watered stock, Pierpont said, after only a quick glimpse at the paper, "I accept this price." After they both signed a contract, Pierpont said, "Mr. Carnegie, I want to congratulate you on being the richest man in the world." Carnegie later admitted to Pierpont that he had sold out too cheap, by $100 million. Not about to spare the industrialist's feelings, Pierpont supposedly replied, "Very likely, Andrew."

The newly formed U.S. Steel was the largest corporation in the world. The giant holding company owned steel mills, blast furnaces, coke ovens, ore mines, barges, steamships, thousands of acres of coke and coal land, and several railroads. It controlled nearly half of America's steel making capacity and produced more than half its total steel output—seven million tons a year. It was the first billion-dollar corporation in history, with a value equal to about seven percent of the U.S. gross national product in 1901. The new corporation earned—and spent—more than the entire U.S. government.

After completing the U.S. Steel merger, Pierpont sailed to France on his yacht. He was now at the peak of his power. He was clearly the undisputed deal maker of the country, if not the western world. He was trusted by the leaders of business and government to do what he said he would do and to act in their best interests. But it was a position that created great envy, and while taking the curative waters at a spa, his company, in the hands of his uncertain lieutenants, was blind sided by the railroad man E. H. Harriman and several merchant bankers. Harriman merged the Union Pacific railroad with the Southern Pacific. Working with the banking house Kuhn, Loeb and the Rockefellers (who had long resented what they saw as Morgan's undermining of Standard Oil's sweetheart rate deals with the railroads), Harriman was determined to prevent Pierpont's interlocking system of investors from controlling the railroads in the Northwest United States.

Harriman decided to take control of the Northern Pacific railroad, which ran from Wisconsin to Seattle. He began by buying $78 million in Northern Pacific stock, the largest such market operation in history at the time. He was able to hide what he was doing for a while by buying the shares in small bunches. But the J.P. Morgan &

Morgan worked with Charles Schwab (left) to create U.S. Steel, the world's largest steel company. *(Courtesy of the Library of Congress.)*

Co. partners eventually caught on to Harriman and cabled Pierpont in France for instructions. In the meantime, they bid frantically to keep Harriman from gaining control of a majority of shares. This drove up the price of the Northern Pacific stock.

The bidding war encouraged speculators to "short" the market. This meant that they borrowed stock from a broker and sold it, with the expectation of repurchasing the stock at a lower price and returning it to the broker. But the price did not come down because no one was selling. Everyone was buying, which drove the price even higher. The Northern Pacific share price rose from $146 to $1,000.

When the original owners of the stock demanded it be returned, the short sellers dumped their other stocks in hopes of raising enough cash to repurchase the inflated railroad stock. This action drove down prices all across the exchange, and the market crashed. The panic of 1901 was on. Before it was over, thousands of investors were bankrupted. Hundreds of speculators—and the brokerage houses from which they had borrowed stock—were saved from financial ruin only because Pierpont convinced Harriman to hold off taking possession of the stock that he had bought. Morgan did the same. Instead, they sold enough shares at $150 to allow the short sellers to cover their debts.

Pierpont had won another stock battle. He was the only man who could both start and stop Wall Street panics.

This cartoon parodies E. H. Harriman's attempts to monopolize the railroad industry.
(Courtesy of the Library of Congress.)

When he returned to the U.S. in July, he installed a new board of Northern Pacific directors that included parties from both sides of the conflict. He was not interested in gloating over his victory and set about devising a plan for permanent railroad peace in the Northwest.

A giant holding company was created to control the securities of the Northern Pacific, the Chicago, Burlington and Quincey, and the Great Northern. Pierpont's lawyer warned him that the plan violated the Sherman Antitrust law because one board would control several competitors that set rates on interstate commerce. Pierpont, more concerned about stable markets than the legality of his actions, ignored the objections. Eventually, the Northern Pacific, Great Northern and Chicago, and Burlington and Quincey lines, were merged into one railroad.

In 1901 alone, J. Pierpont Morgan had been the driving force behind the organization of the world's largest corporation (U.S. Steel), had stopped a corporate raider in his path, and had reorganized the railroad system in the Northwest. He strode around the financial world on both sides of the Atlantic like a giant and was seen by many to be the most powerful man in the world. But the events of the next few years would reveal that he was not immune to pressure and political attack.

The assassination of President McKinley in the fall of 1901 rang a warning bell for Morgan and other giants of the industrial age. With McKinley as president, there had been little antitrust enforcement. But the new president,

Theodore Roosevelt, Jr., had gained publicity during his tenure as governor of New York by his refusal to submit to the demands of big business.

Soon after assuming office, Roosevelt began advocating the reining in of the big trusts. One of the first steps he took was to instruct the U.S. Justice Department to file an antitrust suit against the Northern Securities Company, the recently formed holding company that controlled the Northern Pacific railroad. This prompt action against his newly organized railroad system stunned Pierpont. He met with Roosevelt at the White House. During the meeting he asked the president to send his "man"—the Attorney General—to meet with Pierpont's "man"—his lawyer—to "fix things up." This was how he had done business with politicians before. Roosevelt reacted angrily to the suggestion that he and Morgan had a mere business disagreement and not a deep philosophical divide over the relative power of government and big business. Roosevelt saw that Pierpont did not understand his view that it was important for government to limit corporate power for the good of all the people.

Morgan *was* shocked when Roosevelt would not simply agree to a deal. To Pierpont, these gigantic corporations he assembled were necessary to compete in world markets. Roosevelt's idea was that government should have the necessary power to check financial abuses and to end Wall Street's domination of government economic policy.

In spite of the showdown over Northern Securities, Roosevelt was not Pierpont's enemy. It became evident that the president did not think trusts were all bad when he encouraged J.P. Morgan & Co. to organize an international trust to rule the North Atlantic cargo and passenger ship market. Roosevelt believed that controlling the seas was the key to a nation's military power. He was not timid about asking for Morgan's assistance in creating a trust to buy several British shipping lines, including White Star. In a few short years the White Star Line, once it was in American control, would introduce a new class of passenger ships when it launched the *Titanic*.

In short, Roosevelt was more concerned to establish the government's right to regulate trusts than he was in taking immediate action against existing trusts. He wanted the precedent to be established that corporations, as well as citizens, were all subject to the law of the nation. Although the case against Northern Securities dragged on, and he soon went after the Standard Oil trust of John D. Rockefeller, Roosevelt was not interested in an all out war against big business. He even used advisors from J. P. Morgan & Co. to help set up his new Department of Commerce and Labor. And, unlike his predecessors Hayes and Cleveland, he used a banker—Pierpont—to help settle a coal miners' strike instead of sending in troops. The strike ended peacefully and, under Pierpont's direction, the coal owners for the first time negotiated with representatives from organized labor. It was also the first time the government had maintained a neutral stance in a labor dispute. In earlier strikes, such as the Pullman Strike of 1894, federal troops assisted management in breaking up the strike.

In 1903, a court in Saint Paul, Minnesota, ruled for the federal government's effort to dissolve the Northern Securities Company. The Supreme Court narrowly upheld the decision a year later. The railroads owned by the holding company were given back to their previous owners and left to compete with each other again. But a year later, during the 1904 presidential campaign, the Morgan bank, as if to show that all was forgiven, gave $150,000 toward Roosevelt's reelection. Yet there were enough real philosophical differences remaining that when Roosevelt left for an African safari, Pierpont declared that he hoped the first lion the President met would be his last.

The U.S. Supreme Court's decision about the Northern Securities case did not end the railroad trust. The railroads could still merge into one company instead of forming a system of interlocking boards of directors. This would let them avoid the illegality of coordinating their efforts and prices. Pierpont and the men he had selected still sat on all the boards of directors of the major railroads. After Congress passed a bill to regulate railroads and authorized the Interstate Commerce Commission to set freight rates, Morgan hoped that federal regulation would impose the stability that he had been seeking for decades.

Pierpont eventually made a deal with Roosevelt that eliminated fear of further antitrust prosecutions. He would open the books of any of his companies the Attorney General was suspicious of—and correct anything the Attorney General thought improper. In other words, he and Roosevelt finally agreed for their "men" to get together and solve any problems. Eventually, this deal was made public and set off a firestorm of bad publicity. It seemed that the White House was selling out to big business. Roosevelt refused to apologize. As far as he was concerned, he had developed a sophisticated way to keep the trusts in check.

Chapter Eight

The Big Chief

By 1907, the U.S. economy was once again teetering on the edge of collapse. World production of gold had not kept up with demand. Investment money needed in the United States was being drained away by more attractive interest rates in Europe. The federal treasury had no way to increase the amount of money in circulation and had no mechanism to monitor interest rates. The banks had created a system where they made short term loans to each other to ease cash crunches, but there was nothing to protect banks across the country if each one tried to call in their loans at the same time.

The New York banks were especially dependent on loans from banks around the country. If there was a run on the banks by depositors and the banks began to call in loans the whole system could tumble down. To add to the problem, some New York banks were speculating wildly in copper mining and railroad stocks, and half the bank loans in New York were backed by stocks and bonds. If the stocks and bonds suddenly lost value, then a banking crisis would quickly ripple throughout the economy.

On March 14, the inevitable happened. The pressures on the stock market became too great. Prices collapsed, brokerage houses started to fail, and interest rates soared. Banks began calling in loans.

At first, Pierpont hesitated to get his company involved in a quickly organized effort to prop up the market with $25 million of easily available credit. At seventy, he worked for only an hour or two a day, and he was often gone for months at a time. But he decided to approve the intervention, and his participation was enough to calm the market.

The respite was temporary. As frightened investors traded in their stocks for the safe haven of gold, stock prices continued to fall, more brokerages failed, and bank reserves declined. The market crashed again on August 10, then temporarily stabilized before resuming a downward spiral.

The Panic of 1907 resumed in full force in October. Pierpont was in Richmond, Virginia, attending the Episcopal Church convention, when urgent telegrams from 23 Wall Street caused him to rush back in his private railroad car. On Monday, October 21, the day after his return, the metal and mining companies began to fail after an attempt by one of them to "corner" copper shares, that is, buy up the entire supply, failed. This resulted in a sudden glut of copper, driving down prices. As these shares collapsed, their stock prices followed.

WALL STREET DURING THE BANKING PANIC

WHILE HUNDREDS OF APPREHENSIVE DEPOSITORS THRONGED WALL STREET DURING THE HEIGHT OF LAST WEEK'S DISTURBANCE IN THE FINANCIAL WORLD, OTHER HUNDREDS, LESS VITALLY CONCERNED, WATCHED THE SPECTACLE FROM NEIGHBORING POINTS OF VANTAGE

This news photo appeared in *Harper's Weekly* during the 1907 panic. *(Courtesy of the Archives of The Pierpont Morgan Library, New York.)*

Despite his age and increasing infirmity, Pierpont remained calm and focused on the problem. He could not ignore such an enormous threat to the system. Everyone, rich capitalists like himself and ordinary working people—farmers, workers, and small businessmen—would suffer if the economy fell into depression as it had in 1893. This would be his last hurrah, as he suddenly found himself again, because of the default of everyone else, the central banker of the United States.

His first step was to assemble a team of bankers to report which banks were in such bad shape that they were beyond help and which could be saved. After selecting the ones that could be saved, Pierpont's team, aided by the U.S. Treasury, would pour in money and stop the run on the banks and the sale of stocks. They also audited the books of the trust that had tried to corner the copper market and found its situation hopeless. It was allowed to fail.

The next night, Pierpont and other bankers met with the Secretary of the Treasury, who had been instructed by President Roosevelt to put up $25 million at Pierpont's disposal. Clearly, despite his Northern Securities suit, Roosevelt had the highest regard for J.P. Morgan.

On Wednesday, October 23, Pierpont and two other bankers came up with $3 million by themselves to save another large trust that was on the brink of failing.

As banks outside New York continued to withdraw their reserves from New York, stock prices fell even

President Theodore Roosevelt put Morgan in charge of diverting the Panic of 1907.
(Courtesy of the Library of Congress.)

more. Crowds of people waited in the street in front of his home as Pierpont met day and night with the heads of New York's biggest banks. He would not let them leave until they pledged millions of dollars to save the banks under siege from long lines of depositors waiting to withdraw their money. As Pierpont drove to his office the next day, people shouted: "There goes the Old Man!" and "There goes the Big Chief!"

Despite his around-the-clock efforts, the panic slowed, but did not stop. For two weeks, people camped out in front of their banks, waiting to withdraw their money. Some people paid "standees" to hold their place in line. Elsewhere, the police gave out place-holding numbers. Tellers counted the money as slowly as possible to avoid running out.

Brokers who were about to go bankrupt stopped Pierpont in the street or thronged outside the doors of 23 Wall Street, begging him for help. But even with a $10 million loan from John D. Rockefeller to ease the cash squeeze, the panic continued to spread.

On Thursday, the president of the stock exchange told Pierpont that at least fifty brokers whose money was tied up in the falling market would fail unless he could bail them out with a loan of $25 million. Pierpont quickly assembled the bankers again and raised the money in a mere sixteen minutes. When Pierpont sent a messenger to the floor of the exchange to announce the loans, the crowd of relieved brokers tore the man's coat off. They applauded Pierpont so loudly that he could hear the ovation across the street in his office.

The very next day, the bailing had to start all over again. More loan money was needed at the exchange as stock prices continued to fall. With money in short supply because banks around the country were continuing to pull their money out of the city, Pierpont persuaded the New York Clearing House, where bankers settled their debts with each other, to issue "scrip," promises to pay set amounts of money, as a temporary emergency currency to relieve the cash shortage.

An eyewitness gave this image of Morgan as he left the Clearing House during the panic:

> With his coat unbuttoned and flying open, a piece of white paper clutched tightly in his right hand, he walked fast down Nassau Street, headed back to the bank. His flat topped black derby hat was set firmly down on his head. Between his teeth he held the paper cigar holder in which was one of his long cigars, half smoked. His eyes were fixed straight ahead. He swung his arms as he walked and took no notice of anyone. He didn't seem to see the throngs in the street, so intent was his mind on the thing that he was doing. Everyone knew him, and people made way for him, except some who were equally intent on their own affairs, and these he brushed aside. He didn't dodge, or walk in and out or halt or slacken his pace. He simply barged along, as if he had been the only man going down Nassau Street hill

past the Subtreasury. He was the embodiment of power and purpose . . . Not more than two minutes after he disappeared into his office, the cheering on the floor of the Stock Exchange could be heard out in Broad Street.

Four days later, on Monday, the pace of European money withdrawals had stepped up again. Pierpont had persuaded European banks to put $20 million worth of gold on ships bound for New York, but now a new problem had arisen— saving New York City from bankruptcy. Once again, Pierpont gathered the bankers in the "black library" and persuaded them to buy the city's bonds.

The panic continued all that week as Pierpont and his colleagues rescued banks and helped the stock market stay afloat. Everyone was exhausted after two weeks of crisis and no sleep. Fighting a cold, Pierpont had persuaded, or bullied, or threatened, or ordered to keep money flowing in the markets.

On Friday, November 1, the likely failure of a brokerage house threatened to set off a new round of panic. On Sunday, November 3, at 9:30 p.m., more than fifty men gathered at Pierpont's "balck library." One of them later recalled the "anxious throng of bankers, too uneasy to sit down or converse at ease, pacing through the long marble hall and up and down the high ceilinged rooms" filled with Renaissance bronzes, Gutenberg Bibles, magnificent tapestries, and illuminated manuscripts.

Pierpont locked the doors and kept them in the library

for six hours. The bankers were asked to come up with yet another $25 million to protect the weakest trusts. After hours of bargaining, he confronted his exhausted "guests" at 4:15 in the morning with a statement providing for each trust company to subscribe its share to a new $25 million loan. He pulled each one to the table and waited until they signed.

Meanwhile, Pierpont's associates at U.S. Steel were racing to Washington on a special Pullman car to get government approval to buy another steel company, Tennessee Coal and Iron, which was owned by the broker who had tried to corner the copper market. U.S. Steel was assured by President Roosevelt himself that it would not be prosecuted under the antitrust law if it acquired the other company. It was needed to create more stability in the business. When word of concurrence in the steel company takeover and of the all-night conference at the library became public, the panic finally ended.

Pierpont had reached the zenith of his influence with his actions in the 1907 Panic and the tributes flowed in. But there were many unexpected consequences of his actions, then and later.

For one thing, despite his efforts, the Panic of 1907 caused a depression in which even well-managed businesses failed and people lost their jobs. Without his efforts, of course, it would have been much worse.

The arrangement made with President Roosevelt allowing U.S. Steel to buy the smaller company came back to haunt the politicians and the businessmen. Morgan himself was soon charged with having created the panic in order to buy a rival cheaply and of having tricked Roosevelt. Two congressional investigations over the next four years concluded, after testimony from unreliable witnesses, that a fraud had been perpetrated to the benefit of Pierpont and U.S. Steel. In essence, he was accused of creating the Panic of 1907 for his own benefit.

Roosevelt defended his and Pierpont's actions, and no formal charges came directly from the hearings. It was obvious to independent observers then and later that in the fall of 1907 Pierpont had been worried about sustaining the U.S. economy and not enriching himself. But the public perception had been made and even the fact that the Morgan banks lost $21 million that year did not stop the attacks.

Most importantly, Pierpont's victory persuaded many that the United States could never again allow one independent man to wield such power. The disaster left no doubt that the country needed a central bank, new banking legislation, and currency reform to control these wild contractions in the economy. The money supply must be made flexible and there must be a governmental lender "of last resort." Many thought it was time to make the job J.P. Morgan had been performing into an official government position.

Chapter Nine

On Trial

The Democratic candidate for president in 1908 was Pierpont's old foe, William Jennings Bryan. Once again, Bryan called for stronger laws to regulate the trusts and the railroads, lower tariffs, and increased recognition of union rights. Once again, he painted the "money trust"—meaning Pierpont—as the greatest evil, and denounced President Roosevelt's agreement to the U.S. Steel takeover of Tennessee Coal and Iron that helped to end the Panic of 1907. But once again, Bryan lost the election.

Pierpont was certain that William Howard Taft, the winner of the 1908 election and Roosevelt's chosen heir, would prove friendlier to Wall Street than Roosevelt. But in fact he prosecuted antitrust cases more vigorously, including two Pierpont creations, U.S. Steel and International Harvester, and Rockefeller's Standard Oil trust. Popular hostility to Wall Street was running so high that President Taft, in spite of his personal respect for Pierpont, considered it bad politics to even meet with him.

In November 1910, several Wall Street bankers worked out a plan that reflected Pierpont's design. He advocated a central bank to be kept under private control. The central bank would be interlocked with a system of regional reserve banks run by a governing board of commercial bankers.

When Senator Nelson Aldrich introduced a bill in Congress to create this central banking system, the Democrats blocked it. As much as they hated and feared the "Money Trust," many Democrats and Populists opposed a central bank, fearing it would be dominated by the gold standard men. Wisconsin's Senator Robert W. La Follette, a vocal enemy of the trusts, described Pierpont as "a beefy, red-faced, thick-necked financial bully drunk with wealth and power, [who] bawls his orders to stock markets, directors, courts, governments and nations."

Morose and fatalistic in his last years, Pierpont felt misunderstood by the public and angered by the uproar over his trusts. He shook his cane menacingly at reporters. He was estranged from his daughter Anne, who used her inherited millions for progressive causes.

The "thick-necked financial bully" was now spending his springs in Europe and his summers yachting, therefore he was available to his firm only for a few months in the fall. He revisited the archeological excavations along the Nile that were supplying exhibits for the Metropolitan Museum of Art. In 1909, he was photographed on a small donkey galloping into the Egyptian desert ahead of his flabbergasted guides. He had a steel steamer constructed so he could sail the Nile in his paddle-wheel boat and view the excavations at Khargeh, 400 miles southwest of Cairo.

He was still spending huge sums on his collections. He bought the first two books printed in English by William Caxton in 1474—a history of Troy and a book about chess—and the manuscripts of *Pudd'nhead Wilson* and *Life on the Mississippi* directly from the author, Mark Twain.

Pierpont's last year was filled with calamities. His shipping trust, the International Mercantile Marine, faced stiff competition from the Cunard Line, which had built the swift and luxurious *Mauretania* and *Lusitania* with British government subsidies. To counter Cunard, J. Bruce Ismay of the International Mercantile Marine had decided to build a pair of mammoth ships, *Titanic* and *Olympic*. In May 1911, Pierpont attended the Belfast christening of the *Titanic* and booked a spot on the ill-fated maiden voyage, but had to cancel.

Pierpont was on a lengthy sojourn in Europe the next year when he heard about the *Titanic*'s sinking. The shipping trusts had never been profitable and this disaster unleashed newspaper and political denunciations against both White Star Lines and Pierpont himself. The British-operated, American-owned ship was accused of many deficiencies: an insufficient number of lifeboats, a crew that ignored warnings of icebergs, a poorly organized rescue, even failure to put binoculars in the crow's nest. Newspapers depicted luxurious staterooms laid out for Pierpont and others as proof of a misplaced emphasis on winning wealthy passengers away from Cunard, rather than on safety.

At first Pierpont and his son Jack, who was now in charge of day-to-day operations of J.P. Morgan & Co., defended J. Bruce Ismay, the White Star chairman who disguised himself as a woman and jumped in a lifeboat to save his life. Later, they forced him to resign. Four years later, the White Star Line conceded responsibility for the accident in court and paid out $2.5 million in damages. This forced the shipping trust to default on its bonds.

During that same European visit in 1912, Pierpont and Kaiser Wilhelm, the ruler of Germany and cousin of the King of England, sailed in a yacht race, pulling on the main sheet and sweating with the crew. It was only two years before the beginning of World War I, in which the forces of the Kaiser would eventually be arrayed against those of the European allies—and of America.

While Pierpont was in Europe dealing with the *Titanic* and the Kaiser, the presidential campaign back home was largely focused on bringing down the trusts. Millions of Americans looked at Wall Street and saw only booms and panics, job-killing mergers, and dangerous factories. Newspaper cartoons depicted Morgan as the ultimate selfish tycoon.

Leading the attack against him and the "Money Trust" in Congress was congressman Charles A. Lindbergh, Sr.,

Morgan invested in the doomed *S.S. Titanic*, owned by the White Star Line. *(Courtesy of the Library of Congress.)*

father of the future aviator. On Wall Street, ambitious young investigative reporters nicknamed "muckrakers" examined the elaborate interlocking directorates that controlled the large corporations. One famous reporter, Lincoln Steffens, documented the links between the New York banks and declared that Pierpont was "the boss of the United States."

At the Democratic National convention, three-time presidential candidate William Jennings Bryan fulminated in opposition "to the nomination of any candidate for president who is the representative or under obligation to J. Pierpont Morgan . . . or any other member of the privilege-hunting and favor-seeking class." The eventual Democratic nominee, New Jersey governor Woodrow Wilson, accused Pierpont's friends, the Republicans, of supporting tariffs—taxes on imported goods—to shield the trusts from foreign competition. Calls for financial reform would become a major part of Wilson's campaign.

Pierpont became a divisive figure even among Republicans, and helped to split the party in 1912. Roosevelt was angry with Taft for not continuing his policies. After Roosevelt's calls for environmentalism, "the fair distribution of property," and controls on concentrated power and wealth cost him the Republican presidential nomination, he decided to run as the candidate of a new third party—the Progressive, or Bull Moose, party.

In the general election that November, Roosevelt split the Republican vote and Wilson won, with Taft coming in a poor third. The new chief executive would take office with Democratic majorities in both houses and a clear mandate for reform. He immediately declared war on monopoly concentration, promising to protect American farmers and workers from big business.

Congressman Lindbergh introduced a resolution in the house calling for a congressional probe into the concentration of power on Wall Street. This resulted in the "Pujo" hearings of the House Banking and Currency Committee, named after the subcommittee chairman, Arsene Pujo, which began in December 1912. Pierpont and his friends, colleagues, and partners were to be the star witnesses.

William H. Taft (above) was defeated by Woodrow Wilson in the 1912 presidential election. *(Courtesy of the Library of Congress.)*

Pierpont and his partners decided to take a tough public line during their testimony before the hearing. This was a far different strategy than their usual caution. As a private banker, Pierpont had never felt an obligation to inform the public about his business and had never hired a publicist. But now he was coached for the hearings. Morgan partners met with selected reporters and publishers and contributed articles to influential journals.

Pierpont headed a sixteen person entourage to Washington, including respected ex-government officials and lawyers. The morning of the hearings, the world's most famous banker emerged from a big, high topped limousine and marched up the steps of the Capitol in striped pants, a velvet collared coat, and silk top hat, grasping a cane. An immense crowd ringed the block. In the hearing room he sat erect, but looked tired. He simply could not understand why anyone would question his intentions—or his honesty.

The hearings revealed that seventy-eight major corporations, including many of the country's most powerful holding companies, banked at J.P. Morgan & Co. Pierpont and his partners, in turn, held seventy-two directorships in 112 corporations, spanning the worlds of finance, railroads, transportation, and public utilities. Some banks had so many overlapping directors it was hard to separate them. The banks owned each other's stock. This way the Morgan banks could exercise veto power over new entrants to the capital markets. Eighteen financial institutions effectively controlled capital resources of $25 billion—equal to two-thirds of the entire output of goods and services in the nation.

The Pujo committee's interrogator was a sharp lawyer named Samuel Untermyer. Untermyer asked Pierpont if he was not a large stockholder in another powerful bank, the National City. "Oh no," answered Pierpont, "only about a million dollars' worth." Pierpont seemed surprised when general laughter greeted this response, but after a minute he joined in.

Untermyer wanted to show that New York's leading banks—J.P. Morgan & Co., National City, the First National, Bankers Trust, and Guaranty Trust—had a stranglehold on the country's capital and credit. Pierpont wanted to show the opposite—that there was no such thing as personal control in the complicated business of money.

Where Untermyer saw a vicious system in the hands of a few, Pierpont saw practical solutions to difficult problems. To him, the movement of money in the international system was complicated. There were booms and panics and depressions, price wars and speculations and defaults, and money needed to be carefully directed to create prosperity. When a "Morganization" succeeded, stock prices rose. When a combination failed, all his financial and political efforts could not keep share prices from falling. To him, industrial concentration was a virtual force of nature—irresistible, certainly not invented by him, and better off in his hands than it might have been in others'.

One exchange in particular became famous because it seemed to sum up Pierpont's philosophy in a nutshell:

> Untermyer: "Is not commercial credit based primarily upon money or property?"
>
> Pierpont: "No, sir, the first thing is character."
> Untermyer: "Before money or property?"
>
> Pierpont: "Before money or anything else. Money cannot buy it . . . Because a man I do not trust couldn't get money from me on all the bonds in Christendom."

The audience applauded. In saying this, Pierpont was being neither noble nor cynical—he was merely restating a principle he had learned from his father, and one he had always used as a guide in business dealings.

Pierpont's testimony was well received on Wall Street and by the press and by his family—but some commentators distinguished between honest testimony by a trustworthy man and the potential dangers of control by untrustworthy men. Pierpont was angry that he was even being questioned for using his influence to protect investors against irresponsible management. The committee lawyer, Untermyer, saw Pierpont's testimony as a cover for control of his interests. Pierpont had denied having control of anything.

The Pujo committee eventually concluded that there was not a "conspiracy," in the criminal sense among Morgan and the other "money men." Instead they said it was a "community of interest" that concentrated "the control of credit and money in the hands of a few men" who carefully negotiated deals and then shared the work, and the profits, with other banks.

As a result of the Pujo hearings, in December 1913, President Wilson signed the Federal Reserve Act, providing the government with a central bank overseeing private regional reserve banks, freeing the government of reliance on the House of Morgan in emergencies, and guaranteeing banks around the nation the money they needed to operate.

Chapter Ten

Death of a Titan

The public inquisition of 1912 was too much for the seventy-five-year-old Pierpont. The next year he asked a visitor to assure President Wilson that he would still be of service whenever he was needed. He then left for Egypt, sailing up the Nile one more time. In early February, while on the Nile, he experienced a nervous breakdown. He was afraid he would jump out a window or off the deck of their boat. Nightmares interrupted his sleep. He thought he was going to die, that there was a conspiracy against him, that his whole life's work was wasted. Unable to eat, he was sedated and ordered to bed. The man who had always ignored his critics was now convinced that they were all out to get him, whether over the trusts, his handling of the panics, the loss of the *Titanic*, or anything else he had ever done or not done.

Pierpont finally delegated all executive authority to his son Jack—which showed how tired and sick he felt. He had smoked dozens of cigars daily, eaten huge breakfasts, enjoyed drinking in the evening, and refused to exercise. From boyhood he had been chronically sick, often spending several days in bed each month. Hardly a period of his life had been free of illness and depression. The terrible year of 1912 had finally been too much. The Morgan family, especially Jack, blamed Untermyer, the Pujo Committee's inquisitor, for Pierpont's breakdown.

Pierpont moved on to Rome, where he was met by a battery of doctors from New York. News of Pierpont's illness exploded like a bomb in the art world, which had counted on his purchases to keep prices high. Everyone in Rome who had artwork to sell rushed to the Grand Hotel, where he lay dying. On the morning of March 31, he grew delirious and mumbled about his boyhood, imagining himself back at school in Hartford or Switzerland and saying, "I've got to go up the hill." He died shortly after noon, his daughter Louisa by his side.

Within twelve hours, the Pope and 3,697 other people had telegraphed their regrets to the hotel. Secretary of State William Jennings Bryan, Pierpont's old foe, instructed the American ambassador in Rome to assist the Morgan family in any way he could. The Italian army in Rome marched before Pierpont's coffin, as before a king's. Mourners in Paris covered the coffin with orchids, carnations, roses and palms. French soldiers at Le Havre saluted it with high honors.

Pierpont had left specific instructions for his funeral.

When the casket reached New York, it lay in state in his library on 36th Street under the white pall that had covered Junius's body twenty-three years earlier. He was buried in the family mausoleum in Hartford, Connecticut.

J.P. Morgan was honored by both a memorial service at Westminster Abbey in London and the closing of the New York Stock Exchange. At sea, flags of the shipping trust flew at half mast. His death was enormous news. Newspapers referred to him as "the Napoleon of Wall Street." It was suggested that the last titan had died, and the world of banking would never again see a figure of such scope. Tributes centered on his "rugged honesty and rock ribbed integrity." Theodore Roosevelt praised his "sincerity and truthfulness," the *Wall Street Journal* praised his "first-class mind," the *London Times* his "distinctly wholesome" influence on the stability of international finance. Others called him an uncrowned monarch and the "embodiment of the heroic age in American industrial history." Even some of Pierpont's critics said he was a builder and conservator, not a wrecker, liar, or cheat.

Joseph Pulitzer's *New York World* newspaper called him the "commanding figure" of a moribund financial feudalism:

> Never again will conditions of government make it possible for any financier to bestride the country like a Colossus . . . Having greater force, greater character, greater intellect and greater vitality than any other man

in Wall Street, he naturally became the leader, and he remained the leader . . . The system he built up with so much skill and effort is doomed to crumble . . . In time little will remain except the feeling of bewilderment that a self-ruling people should ever have allowed one man to wield so much power for good or evil over their prosperity and general welfare, however much ability and strength and genius the man possessed.

Even the Congressional interrogator his family blamed for his death, Samuel Untermyer, told the press: "Whatever may be one's view of the perils to our financial and economic system of the concentration of the control of credit, the fact remains, and is generally recognized, that Mr. Morgan was animated by high purpose and that he never knowingly abused his almost incredible power."

At his death his estate was worth about $80 million, or about $1.2 billion in today's dollars. The value of his art collection was estimated at $50 million—$750 million today. Still, his fortune did not approach those of the great industrialists—Carnegie, Rockefeller, Ford, or Harriman. He bequeathed control of the bank to Jack as well as most of his property, including the Morgan Library, his English houses, the *Corsair*, positions in New York cultural institutions, wine cellars, and cigars. His widow and daughters received large sums in trust. Every J. P. Morgan employee received a year's salary. The thirty-four-page will left money to dozens of family members, friends, and associates and employees and institutions of all kinds. But it said nothing about his vast art collection. Jack eventually sold some of it to pay inheritance taxes and gave much of the rest, other than what was on display at the Morgan Library, to the Metropolitan Museum of Art.

Ultimately, J. Pierpont Morgan must be judged by the times he lived in. The "Napoleon of Wall Street" did not operate only to make money for himself, but out of a patriotic idea of bringing prosperity for all by creating a stable economic system that would, so far as was possible, eliminate the boom and bust cycles, the price wars, the waste and the wild speculation of unbridled competition. The work he did was understood by few, but his weapons—quick access to information, respect on both sides of the Atlantic, and a moral sense that what was good for Wall Street was good for America—made him the informal central banker of the United States for the critical years of the industrial revolution.

Timeline

1837—Born in Hartford, Connecticut on April 17.

1850—Moves to Boston.

1854—Graduates from Boston English. Goes to school in Switzerland.

1856—Attends University of Göttingen, Germany.

1857—Moves to New York City.

1861—Marries Amelia Sturges on October 7.

1862—Amelia dies on February 17. Forms J.P. Morgan & Company in September.

1865—Marries Frances Louisa Tracy on May 31.

1869—Defends Albany and Susquehanna railroad from raiders.

1885—Negotiates the Great Railroad Treaty.

1895—Establishes a system to exchange U.S. bonds for gold, diverting a currency crisis.

1901—Creates U.S. Steel and Northern Securities Company.

1904—U.S. Supreme Court orders dissolution of Northern Securities Company.

1907—Organizes investors to end bank panic.

1912—Testifies before the U.S. House Pujo Committee investigating the power of the "money trust."

1913—Dies in Rome on March 31. Federal Reserve Board established in December.

Sources

Chapter One—Banker's Son

p. 9, "You felt something electric . . ." Jean Strouse, *Morgan, American Financier*, (New York: Random House, 1999), xii.

p. 14, "converse with the fair damsels" Ibid., 36.

Chapter Three—Family Business

p. 34, "just in from a fight with other Indians . . ." Strouse, *American Financier*, 132.

p. 39, "of excellent character . . ." Ibid., 137.

Chapter Four—Nation's Banker

p. 44, "Mr. Morgan, do you take one lump or two in your nose?" Strouse, *American Financier*, xii.

p. 49, "I put my hand on Ramses' skull." Ibid., 204.

p. 53, "Think of it . . ." Ibid., 306.

p. 53, " 'Railroad Kings Form a Gigantic Trust' " Ibid., 306.

Chapter Five—Dodging a Panic

p. 60, "Jewish bankers and British gold . . ." Strouse, *American,* 349.

p. 61, "You shall not press down . . ." Ibid., 356.

Chapter Seven—U.S. Steel

p. 84, "Mr. Carnegie, I want to congratulate you . . ." Ron Chernow, *The House of Morgan*, (New York: Touchstone, 1990), 84.

Chapter Eight—The Big Chief

p. 84, "There goes the Old Man!" Strouse, *American Financier*, 579.

p. 85, "With his coat unbuttoned . . ." Herbert L. Satterlee, *J. Pierpont Morgan, An Intimate Portrait*, (New York: Macmillan Co. 1939), 479, quoted in Strouse, *American Financier*, 580.

p. 86, "anxious throng of bankers . . ." Strouse, *American Financier*, 586.

Chapter Nine—On Trial

p. 90, "a beefy, red-faced, thick-necked financial . . ." Strouse, *American Financier*, x.

p. 93, "the boss of the United States." Ibid., 594.

p. 93, "to the nomination of any candidate . . ." Ibid., 664.

p. 97, "only about a million dollars' worth . . ." Ibid., 10.

p. 98, "Is not commercial credit . . ." Ibid., 13.

p. 99, "the control of credit and money . . ." Chernow, *Intimate Portrait*, 155.

Chapter Ten—Death of a Titan

p. 101, "I've got to go up the hill." Chernow, *Intimate Portrait* 158.

p. 102, "the Napoleon of Wall Street." Ibid., 160.

p. 102, "rugged . . . in American industrial history." Strouse, *American Financier*, 15.

p. 102, "Never again will conditions of . . ." Ibid., 15.

p. 103, "Whatever may be one's view . . ." Ibid., 15.

Bibliography

Auchincloss, Louis. *J.P. Morgan: The Financier As Collector.* New York: Harry N. Abrams, 1990.

Brands, H.W. *Masters of Enterprise: Giants of American Business from John Jacob Astor and J.P. Morgan to Bill Gates and Oprah Winfrey.* New York: Free Press, 1999.

Chernow, Ron. *The House of Morgan.* New York: Simon & Schuster, Inc., 1990.

Lamont, Thomas W. *Henry P. Davison: The Record of a Useful Life.* New York: Harper & Brothers, 1933.

Laughlin, Rosemary. *John D. Rockefeller: Oil Baron and Philanthropist.* Greensboro, NC: Morgan Reynolds Publishers, 2001.

Satterlee, Herbert. *J. Pierpont Morgan, An Intimate Portrait.* New York: MacMillan Company, 1939.

Strouse, Jean. *Morgan, American Financier.* New York: Random House, 1999.

Index

B
MORGAN

Byman, Jeremy,
1944-

J.P. Morgan, banker
to a growing
nation.

48165

$21.95

DATE		
JAN 26 2007		
DEC 2 2 2010		
FEB 2 2 2011		